Position of Safety

Position of Safety

Sit in a Safe Position

A Supportive Guide for Educators and Childcare Providers

Maria J. Beal Ross

Position of Safety
Sit in a Safe Position

Always Think
Safety First

Words and Actions

FOR

Day Care Providers
Home Care Providers
Head Start Programs
Pre-Kindergarten Programs
(Pre-Kindergarten through Higher Education)
Private & Public Educational Systems
Educators Professional
Health Care Providers Specialist
And any & all agencies that support the needs of children
(All Stakeholders)

Contents

Encouragement

All children deserve to be safe, treated with respect, and proper care in a loving environment. These environments should support academia, language development, social-emotional development, and cognitive & physical development while implementing supportive terminology when working with diverse children in a group setting. Using positive (language) communication that is not discriminative in nature is important. Use terminology that interconnects equity and equality while interacting with different ethnicities of children. It is a must to encourage, strengthen, motivate, support, and build positive self-esteem in all children. Speak with words that represent respect and recognize the cultural diversity of children that are being serviced and/or taught by all who support the needs of children, including that of our colleagues, guardians, and parents.

Think Safety First

Know the etymology of words and their meaning

Be aware of using words that can be:

- Culturally offensive
- Discriminative
- Religious (not separating church and state)
- Ideology of words that prefer certain groups of people

Sitting

Sitting is a natural action performed by humans for centuries. Humans have natural capabilities for sitting. We enjoy sitting outside as well as sitting inside our homes, alone or with our loved ones.

Before furniture was invented, we sat on large rocks, falling trees, dirt floors, grassy fields & meadows, and tree stumps. There is a proper way for sitting when protecting our backs. That is a discussion I leave for the medical professionals to address.

There are many different purposes for sitting, as follows:

- to eat and drink;
- to work and relax;
- to celebrate and collaborate;
- while waiting to be seen;
- to play board games & gaming systems;
- to read, play musical instruments, and watch television;
- for seminars, instructions, concerts & plays;
- we sit at our elder's feet;

- we have sit-ins when fighting against unjust laws and the negative treatment of others;
- we sit to rest our bodies.

Sitting is something everyone can do. It does not discriminate against any ethnicity of people until words that are negative and do not align with equity or equality are applied to it.

Conflict of Words for Sitting

There is a war of words that has stumped educators as of today.

When instructing children throughout the daily educational routine of the classroom, building spoken words (communication) matters. There are no words being used that communicate, represent or match the action of sitting in an educational setting. While educators are disputing which is the appropriate terminology that should be used while encouraging children to sit, negative terminology of words are still in effect. These conflicts of words do not align appropriately with serving culturally and ethnically diverse groups of children in a learning environment. The problem is not understanding how to sit down; the problem is that the language that is being communicated does not represent *equity* or *equality*.

Words should be spoken and understood when serving a culturally diverse children's learning environment. While educators are disputing which is the appropriate terminology that should be used while encouraging children to sit, this issue is still in effect. There are culturally diverse groups of children who continue to experience historical trauma through the use of offensive words.

We, as educators, may be unaware of the harm we cause children by not understanding cultural diversity and words that are offensive. The presentation of spoken words must employ language strategies that support multiculturalism.

Children naturally sit down during certain activities and special events. For example, sitting on the floor for story-time. The problem is that the words that are being used to encourage children to sit on the floor and the actions do not match the words given except for *sit*. The terminology of words does not support the diversity of children in education.

Children are amazing, intelligent, gifted, smart, creative, and talented. They comprehend instruction given by educators differently when spoken. There are children who are in need of unique instruction that requires different forms of pedagogy instruction. Nevertheless, verbiage matters through all educational environments and transitions throughout the day. Using words that are positive and non-offensive is a must.

When encouraging children to sit down on the floor, the following terminology of words are used: sit **criss-cross applesauce**, sit like a **pretzel**, sit **Indian** style, sit like **Buddha,** and sit **yoga** style. These terminologies are used by educators pre-K through higher education and many other establishments that services children. These terminologies (verbiage) do not match or support the pedagogic instructions, cultural diversities, equity, or equality when modeling the action for sitting in the learning environment.

Researching the meanings of words used in a children's learning environment often fails to capture the significance of cultural diversity. When educating a diverse group of children within the daily routines of classroom settings, the choice of spoken words becomes crucial. Currently, the words being employed do not reflect the concept of safety, which should correspond with the physical action of sitting in an educational environment.

The first two phrases of words (sit **criss-cross applesauce** and sit like a **pretzel**) are words that reference food. If these words were given to newly enrolled children of different ethnicities and cultures, the language would not be understood. Unless the action is demonstrated, the communication is not comprehended. Words should be understood when communicating and servicing a learning environment with culturally diverse children.

criss-cross: *noun*
a pattern intersecting straight lines or paths
adjective (of pattern)
containing a number of straight lines or paths that intersect each other
verb
form a pattern of intersecting lines or paths
applesauce: *noun*
1. a puree of stewed apples 2. (Informal-North American) nonsense
pretzel: *noun*
a crisp biscuit baked in the form of a knot or stick with salt,
verb
(North American) twist, bend, or contort

About the next phrase of words, "sit **Indian** style": *Indian* is a terminology given by Christopher Columbus, who thought he had reached the Indies but landed in America. *Indian style* is a negative representation of people who live in India. The term is culturally offensive to aboriginals (indigenous) of this land. Their way of life has been affected by prejudices of the past and present day. These words do not represent inclusiveness. The terminology of these words does not respect nor represent the cultural diversity or ethnicity of children. As of today, the word aboriginal people is considered offensive in Canada, and the word native is accepted[1].

The phrases sit **Buddha** style and **yoga** style represent a religion and spiritual belief. Using these terminologies in religions and spiritual references is showing preferential treatment for individual(s) or a certain group of children. This can cause a door of conflict to manifest between children in a learning environment. Disruption in the learning environment obstruct the educator's instruction time and children's learning time.

Although there are different terminologies (words) used to signal a child to sit with their legs inward, this does not represent cultural diversity. The language being spoken for sitting does not promote safety or support all cultural diversities.

Communicating with children should not be offensive, discriminative, preferring a religion, or preferring an ideology. Communicating with children should not have any negative connotations. Negative words hurt.

There should be a positive terminology of words that do not cause mental and emotional anguish. A nurturing learning environment builds strong self-esteem (resilience) for all ethnicity of children. We are investing life skills in the life of children by teaching them to think about safety first in words and actions. Positive terminology of words should be used that doesn't cause mental or emotional harm, and supports all ethnicities of children.

Language Communication Solution

The United States is known as the great melting pot, a country that has been built by many different ethnicities. Education plays a significant role in the lives of children, emphasizing its importance as a major aspect of their growth and development. It has been expressed by many people that education opens doors of opportunities for all children. These same children will one day grow up to be adults living and working in society throughout the world. The spoken words used with children should always be positive.

Words are always changing, and meaning changes within certain ethnicities. We need to understand the difference between semantics meaning of words from etymology meaning of words. Semantics words have several different meanings. The study of etymology reveals the word's original origin and its historical development. The true meaning of the language we speak in the educational environment is important. It will help us to understand and improve social emotional relationships within the educational settings when interacting with children and their families. This will encourage parent engagement and parent involvement in our schools. There are words that label others that have caused historical trauma and are still forced upon native people. Those who educate and support children should understand the etymology of words and their meanings. We should use words that do not cause stress activation in children, in order to promote positiveness.

It is imperative that we use terminology of words that is not a cause of racial disparity occurrences in any learning environment. Introducing and communicating words should be positive and motivate us to think about keeping ourselves and others safe. Providing quality care for children consists of loving and kind words. Children will model and respond to languages that support self-discipline, self-management and social awareness.

Although there are many types of dialect (languages) around the world, *Position of Safety / Sit In A Safe Position* does not cause confusion among a multicultural global society; it teaches children a multiple step process: 1st. sit down, 2nd. bend your knees outward, 3rd. pull your legs inward, 4th. cross the ankles, and 5th. place your hands on your lap.

Position of Safety / Sit In A Safe Position is using supportive terminology that will motivate and support educators to continue researching and implementing positive approaches to learning, implementing positive collaboration with parents and other educational professionals. Cognitive development of all ethnicities of children is essential. We should never compromise the importance of positive communication when it comes to educating our children. Communication and language is something that we will continue to use throughout our childhood to adulthood.

These words line up with what educators and others believe to be positive communication for children. The language supports positive interaction through the use of words that motivates children to listen to the instructions. The words spoken acknowledge and respect the cultural diversity of children. In other words, cultural competency is a must when working with children.

We just don't think education is enough. Being safe creates a strong and productive learning environment.

Preventing children from experiencing bodily injuries supports the need of children while in the care of others. The words spoken *sit in a safe position* line up with equity, equality, and cultural diversities while teaching children and adults to think safety first while sitting. Using this terminology of words reminds children the multiple step process mentioned before. Children in the learning environments are of different ethnicities and may speak different languages. These words does not belittle or have a negative effect on one's self-esteem. Children will automatically remember to keep their hands and feet safe from injury, including their fingers.

Sit in the Position of Safety / Sit In A Safe Position should be introduced at the beginning of the school year, and demonstrated by the educators. All children do not learn the same language or may speak another one. Icons and posters should be posted with the words *Sit in the Position of Safety / Sit In A Safe Position*. If a child speaks another language, their spoken language should be implemented with American English. It is a form of scaffolding when using icons, posters, other participants and their original language. It shows the children and others there is no respect for persons or groups of people. These words build a positive relationship with parents, educators and children.

When a new child enters the learning environment, it should be introduced by the educators and allow other children to share the terminology and demonstrate the words in action. The same communication (language) words should be used collaboratively from one classroom to the next classroom through all learning environments. Educators have many concerns. For example: Cultural Literacy and American Diversity.

The goal of educators is to promote excellence in the learning environment. It shows educators and childcare providers always striving to keep children safe at all times while providing services. Just as preventive (medical) care reduces illness, there should be positive terminology used to remind children and motivate them to think safety first as a preventative care action from bodily injuries. These words build self-esteem while supporting and providing their needs in the education environment. There are words that show in action, "I care about the full overall well-being of children."

As we delve further into the realm of safety education, the impact of our choice of words becomes increasingly significant to avoid confusion in a multicultural society. Considering it teaches children the multiple-step process (1st sit down, 2nd bend knees outward, 3rd pulling your lower legs inward toward your body, 4th crossing legs at the ankles, and 5th place your hands on your lap), this could be used as a mathematical activity (counting, addition, subtraction).

There are many lessons and discussions concerning the word *safety*. Why do we have fire drills, tornado drills, intruder drills? These words could be applied during tornado drills. This should lead to deeper discussion and communication about our community safety workers. It is not enough to have an open-ended discussion but to have a deep conversation about the importance of safety. All of these discussions can be used in all areas of learning development: Why safety is important? What number do we call for emergencies? Educators can use this topic for the discussion of Pedestrian Safety.

There are many different children's books on safety. Examples: *Staying Safe at School, Safety on the Playground, Pedestrian Safety, and ABCs and 123's of Child Safety*. Including *The Three Little Pigs* and *Goldilocks and the Three Bears* with *Little Red*

Riding Hood, advise against talking to strangers. Everyone is concerned with gun safety as well as using technology safely.

The building of an enclave of safety measures for children throughout the learning ecosystem aligns with quality care and minimizing dangerous accidents. Safety precautions being in place throughout children's educational experience shows we value parents' concerns for their children's livelihood. The *Position of Safety/Sit In A Safe Position* represents safety for all children (people). These words support the needs of children's mental and emotional well-being, as well as equity, equality, cultural diversities, and ethnicities of all children. Including families.

Just as we should not tell children to shut-up. It is rude and disrespectful to speak negative words in the learning environment. Offensive words cause negative responses. Using positive words teaches children to speak positively to educators and their peers. These words do not represent the preferential treatment of any ethnicities or religious groups. It is unbiased. They are not culturally offensive.

These words line up with what educators and others know to be positive communication for children. The language supports positive interaction through the use of words that motivates children to listen to educators' instruction. Educators always remind children to listen and pay attention to the words (spoken) communicated during the transition on field trips. There are rules for safely getting on and off school transportation. Bus drivers have practiced emergency bus evacuation too. The words *Position of Safety/Sit In A Safe Position* acknowledge and respect the cultural diversity of children. Changing negative narratives to communicate positive (safety) narrative is beneficial in all educational environments.

We just don't think education is enough. Being safe creates a strong and productive learning environment.

Preventing children from experiencing bodily injuries

supports the needs of children, while in care of others. When a child knows that they are in a safe environment and positive words are spoken, they will want to hear and participate in the learning environment.

The history of education was not presented or shared with support of multiculturalism as a major importance of respecting the life of all children. Administrators should think about implicit bias attitudes and behaviors not being allowed in any educational environments that service children. This is negative communication. It teaches children to speak negatively to their peers as well as others. Children copy what they see and hear. We as educators shoulder a lot of responsibilities. Eyes are always on us. We should strive to be multicultural advocates while serving children of different ethnicities.

Reminding ourselves the words spoken *Sit In A Safe Position* line up with the importance of the social skills of children being developed. Positive communication fosters mental resilience, emotional strength, and strong relationships between children and teachers, teachers and parents, educators and their peers, as well as within their broader community. Teaching children of a diverse learning environment and the diversity of educators to think safety first while sitting. Using the terminology of words that reminds children and adults to bring their legs inward, cross them at the ankles, and immediately place their hands on their lap. That is the meaning of *sitting in a position of safety and sitting in a safe position.*

Position of Safety
Posición de Seguridad

Sitting In A Safe Position
Sesión En UNA Posición

Position of Safety
위치 ~의 안전

Sitting In A Safe Position
좌석 ~안에 ㅏ 안전한 위치

The Etymology of the Words
Position of safety

Sit in a Safe position

LEARNING THE ETYMOLOGY OF WORDS TEACHES THE HISTORY of words and where they originated. It informs us about the origin of words. Clarity of a word is important because all words do not represent or may not communicate the same meaning for all ethnicities throughout the world.

There is so much cultural diversity among the masses of people.

The Etymology of Words
for Positive Communication

Position: *The meaning "place occupied by a person or thing." especially proper or appropriate place.*

Safety: *(n) early 14c. savete, "freedom or immunity from harm or danger; an unharmed or uninjured or uninjured state or condition."*

Sit: *Old English, sittan, "to occupy a seat, be seated, sit down, seat oneself; remain, continue."*

Safe: *adj. C 1 300, sauf, "unscathed, unhurt, uninjured: free from danger or molestation, in safety, secure; etc."*

These words support positive communication and do not discriminate. It is not offensive or biased. These words build bridges with added cohesiveness and unity for a diverse group of children. Children will remind their classmates to sit in the position of safety. Using positive words minimizes challenges and conflict in the learning environment. Using negative communication stigmatizes children.

We cannot see children's (individual) thoughts but we can see the product of thought from facial expressions, body gestures, and behaviors. Children cannot always express when they are feeling mentally and emotionally stressed, or when they are experiencing an anxiety attack. Even adults have issues in this area. Positive words will help de-escalate aggressive behaviors and negative behaviors in the classrooms.

A mentally and physically safe environment for learning puts a smile on their faces. When children are happy and feel safe, they develop a strong sense of themselves. Children develop strong self-esteem, respect, and concern for the safety of both themselves and others. Recognizing the significance of their roles in the learning environment and society can contribute significantly. Knowing the Etymology of words is a supportive tool for educators and students. As an instructional tool educators and all stakeholders should have access to reference materials that support language for multiculturalism.

Let using positive words be a strategy against negative behaviors, aggressive behaviors, and ethnic (racial) insensitive language communication.

Positive reinforcement produces positive outcomes.

Defining Implicit Bias

Also known as implicit social cognition, *IMPLICIT BIAS* refers to the attitudes or stereotypes that affect our understanding, actions, and decisions in an unconscious manner. These biases, which encompass both favorable and unfavorable assessments, are activated involuntarily and without an individual's awareness or intentional control. Residing deep in the subconscious, these biases are different from known biases that individuals may choose to conceal for the purposes of social and/or political correctness. Rather, implicit biases are not accessible through introspection.

The implicit associations we harbor in our subconscious cause us to have feelings and attitudes about other people based on characteristics such as race, ethnicity, age, and appearance. These associations develop over the course of a lifetime beginning at a very early age through exposure to direct and indirect messages. In addition to early life experiences, the media and news programming are often-cited origins of implicit associations.

A Few Key Characteristics of Implicit Biases:

- Implicit biases are pervasive. Everyone possesses them, even people with avowed commitments to impartiality such as judges.

- Implicit and explicit biases are related but distinct mental constructs. They are not mutually exclusive and may even reinforce each other.

- The implicit associations we hold do not necessarily align with our declared beliefs or even reflect stances we would explicitly endorse.

- We generally tend to hold implicit biases that favor our own ingroup, though research has shown that we can still hold implicit biases against our ingroup.

- Implicit biases are malleable. Our brains are incredibly complex, and the implicit associations that we have formed can be gradually unlearned through a variety of debiasing techniques.

Source: Kirwan Institute for the study of Race and ethnicity, State of the Science, at kirwaninstitute.osu.edu/

Implicit biases (plural) - is bias or prejudice that is present but not consciously held or recognized.

Source: merriam-Webster.com

Implicit prejudice: A negative attitude, of which one is not conscious aware, a specific social group. Compare explicit prejudice.

Source: dictionary.apa.org

Etymology Definition

etymonline.com
English

*Bias (v.) "giving a bias to, causing to incline to one side," 1610
literal; 1620's figurative; from bias (n.) compare French biaster.
Related: Diased; biasing*

*Equity (n.) Early 14c equate, "quality of being equal or fair, impar-
tiality, "late 14c, that which is equally right or just to all
concerned," from Old French equite (13c) from Latin aequitatens
(nominative acquitas) "the uniform relatran of one thing to others,
equality, comformity, symmetry." "also just or equitable conduct
toward others,' from aequus" even, just, equal".*

*Equality (n.) Late 14c, "eveness, smoothness, uniformity," c.1400
reference to amount or number; from Old French equality "equality, parity" (Modern French eqalite; similarity, equal" (see equal
(adj)). Early 15c. As "state of being equal." Of privileges, rights,
etc., is English from 1520s.*

Etimología Definición

etymonline.com
Español (Spanish)

Inclinación (v) - "dar un sesgo a, hacer que se incline hacia un lado", 1610 literal; figurativo de 1620; de bias (n). Comparar biaster francés. Relacionado: Sesgado; sesgo

equidad (n) - temprano 14c., equitativo, "cualidad de ser igual o justo, imparcialid ad; finales del 14c., "lo que es igualmente correcto o justo para todos los interesados", del francés antiguo equite (13c) de Latinaequitatens (nominativo acquitas) "la relación uniforme de una cosa con otras, igualdad, conformidad, simetría", también "justo o igualdad, conformidad, simetría" también "conducta justa o equitativa hacia los demás", de aequus " incluso, justo, igual".

igualdad (n) - Finales del 14 c., "uniformidad, suavidad, uniformidad"; C. 1400 referencia a cantidad o número; del francés antiguo equalite "igualdad, paridad" (Francés moderno 'egalité, similitud, igual" (ver igual (adj.)). Principios del 15c como "estado de igual-dad". de privilegios, derechos, etc., es inglés de 1520.

어원 정의

etymonline.com
한국인 (Korean)

편견 (v.) "편향을 주다, 한쪽으로 기울게 하다,' 1610 문자; 1620's 비유; from bias (n). French biaser 비교. 관련 항목; Biased: 편향

형평성 (n) 초기 14c equite, "동등하거나 공정한 평등, 공평함, " 14c 후반, "모든 관련자에게 동등하게 옳거나공정한 tht, "오래된 프랑스어로부터 equite (13c) 라틴어 aequitatens (명목적 acquitas) "the 한 사물과 다른 사물의 균일한 관계, 평등, 동조, 대칭, " 또한 " 다른 사람에 대한 정당하거나 공평한 행위", aequus의' 평등한, 공정한, 동등한'

평등 (n) 후기 14c, "평평함, 매끄러움, 균일성"; c.1400 양 또는수에 대한 참조; Old French equalite "equality, parity, prity" (Modern French eglite; similarity, equal"(equal (adj.) 참조). 15세기 초 "동등한 상태" 로 영어로 1520년대부터 특권, 권리 등

Notes

Conflict of Words for Sitting

1. thecanadianencyclopedia.ca/en/article/indian-term

References

- etymology.com/search
- thecanadianencyclopedia.ca/en/article/indian-term
- umass.edu/legal/derrico/shoshane/indian.htm